Retire Simply

T.S. AVINI

Retire Simply

Secure Your Future with Less Complexity

by T.S. AVINI

Table of Contents

Chapter 1: Understanding the Basics of Retirement Planning

Retirement planning is a journey, as personal as the fingerprints that mark our daily lives.

Whether you're approaching your golden years or still early in your career, understanding the fundamentals of planning for retirement is key to securing a future that doesn't just meet your basic needs but supports a lifestyle you envision. This chapter is dedicated to unraveling the complexities of retirement planning so you can approach it with confidence and clarity.

The Importance of Starting Early

I've seen this happen before: One of the foremost principles of retirement planning is starting early. Time is your greatest ally.

The sooner you begin, the more you can benefit from the power of compounding interest, which Albert Einstein famously referred to as the "eighth wonder of the world. " Compounded interest allows your investment earnings to generate their own earnings, exponentially growing your savings over time.

For example, if a 25-year-old starts investing $200 per month into a retirement account with a 7% annual return, they could potentially accumulate over $500,000 by the age of 65.

However, if they wait until 35 to start saving the same amount monthly, they might end up with only around $245,000. This dramatic difference underscores the critical advantage of beginning your retirement planning as soon as possible.

Setting Goals for Your Retirement

To be honest, Understanding what you want from your retirement is vital. It's not enough to assume that being retired will automatically bring happiness and fulfillment.

Take time to visualize your retirement lifestyle. Will you travel? Spend time with family? Pursue hobbies or volunteer work? Once you have a clearer picture, you can translate those desires into financial goals.

A helpful method in setting these goals is the SMART criteria: Specific, Measurable, Achievable, Relevant, and Time-bound.

Instead of vaguely planning to "save enough" for retirement, a SMART goal could be, "Save $1 million by age 65 to cover estimated annual expenses of $40,000 after Social Security. ".

Understanding Retirement Accounts

I've seen this happen before: Retirement accounts are crucial tools in your financial plan.

They not only provide a disciplined way of saving but also offer tax advantages that can dramatically affect your nest egg. Familiarize yourself with some of the most common types:.

1. **401(k) Plans:** Offered by many employers, a 401(k) lets you save pre-tax dollars, which means you don't pay taxes on your contributions until you withdraw them upon retirement.

Many employers offer matching contributions, essentially free money for your retirement. For example, if your employer matches 50% of up to 6% of your salary, you'd be wise to contribute at least 6% to maximize this benefit.

2. **Individual Retirement Accounts (IRAs):** If a 401(k) isn't an option, an IRA is a great alternative.

Traditional IRAs function similarly to 401(k)s in tax treatment, while Roth IRAs offer tax-free withdrawals in retirement, assuming certain conditions are met. Deciding between the two often comes down to whether you expect to be in a higher tax bracket now or in retirement.

Believe it or not, 3.

Pension Plans: Though less common these days, pensions offer a fixed income in retirement, usually based on salary and years of service. If you're entitled to a pension, understand how it integrates with other income sources.

Each account type has rules and limits, so it's beneficial to discuss options with a financial advisor to determine which blend best suits your retirement plan.

Estimate Your Retirement Needs

I've seen this happen before: Determining how much you'll need for retirement can feel daunting, but breaking it down into steps makes it manageable. Start by estimating your retirement expenses.

Consider basics such as housing, utilities, and food, alongside discretionary expenses like travel and leisure. Don't forget healthcare, which frequently requires a larger portion of retirees' budgets than anticipated.

A common rule of thumb is to aim for 70-80% of your pre-retirement income to maintain your lifestyle.

Suppose you earn $70,000 annually before retirement; you'll likely need $49,000 to $56,000 per year in retirement. Tools and calculators are available online to assist in personalizing these estimates.

Diversification: The Key to Mitigating Risk

As strange as it sounds, Investing for retirement isn't without risk, but diversification is a powerful tool to manage that risk.

The concept is simple: Don't put all your eggs in one basket. Spread your investments among different asset types—stocks, bonds, real estate, and others—to reduce the impact of any single asset's poor performance on your overall portfolio.

Adjust your strategy as you age.

Younger individuals can afford to take more risks for potentially higher returns, while those closer to retirement should focus on preserving capital, favoring stable investments.

The Role of Social Security

I've seen this happen before: Social Security serves as a critical component of most Americans' retirement income.

However, it's essential to understand its role as a supplement rather than the foundation of your retirement plan. The average monthly benefit, as of 2023, is around $1,500—typically not enough to cover all retirement expenses.

You can begin claiming Social Security benefits as early as age 62, but your monthly benefits will increase the longer you wait, up to age 70.

Consider your health, employment, and financial needs when deciding when to start taking benefits. Projection tools are available to help estimate your future benefits based on current earnings and age.

Plan for the Unexpected

Finally, resilience and flexibility are vital in retirement planning.

Life is full of surprises, and your retirement plan should account for the unexpected. This might include building an emergency fund, considering long-term care insurance, or ensuring you have a will in place.

Unexpected events can also be positively life-changing, like a sudden inheritance or a windfall from a sale.

Have a plan that allows you to adapt to such opportunities without discarding your long-term goals.

In closing, the path to retirement should not provoke anxiety, but a sense of purpose.

By understanding the basics, you take control, simplify complexities, and open doors to security and freedom in your golden years. Retirement planning is more than financial preparation; it's a commitment to a future that reflects your values and dreams—one you can confidently look forward to enjoying.

Chapter 2: Setting Realistic Retirement Goals

Retirement planning is often likened to charting a course for a distant destination. Much like sailors in the age of exploration, individuals preparing for retirement must navigate through uncertainty, ever-changing circumstances, and myriad potential pitfalls.

However, unlike those sailors of old, we have the advantage of modern tools and strategies that can simplify our journey significantly. In this chapter, we will explore how to set realistic retirement goals, a fundamental step in ensuring your future is both secure and fulfilling.

Understanding the Importance of Goals

I've seen this happen before: The first step in setting realistic retirement goals is understanding why they're critical. Without well-defined targets, your retirement planning can easily become a journey without direction.

Goals provide clarity and focus, acting as a compass that guides financial decisions and lifestyle choices. They give you a framework to measure progress and adjust plans as needed. Essentially, these goals are the benchmarks against which you'll measure your readiness and ability to retire comfortably.

Envisioning Your Retirement

Before we delve into specifics, take a moment to visualize what retirement means to you. The concept of retirement has evolved significantly over the years.

Gone are the days when it solely meant lounging on beaches or endless games of golf. Today, retirement can involve pursuing passions, starting new businesses, traveling, volunteering, or taking up new hobbies. Your vision for retirement will heavily influence your goals, so it's important to define it clearly.

At first glance, Start by asking yourself some key questions: What does a typical day in retirement look like for you? Where do you want to live? What activities will you pursue? Do you plan to continue working in some capacity? Your answers will help shape personalized goals that reflect your desired lifestyle.

Calculating Your Financial Needs

Once you have a clear vision, the next step is to translate that vision into financial terms. This involves calculating the amount of money you'll need to sustain your desired lifestyle.

Begin by estimating basic living expenses, such as housing, utilities, groceries, transportation, and healthcare. Don't forget to include leisure activities, travel, and any other expenses related to your hobbies or desired lifestyle.

I've seen this happen before: It's also crucial to account for inflation.

The cost of living is likely to rise over the years, and failing to factor this into your calculations can lead to significant shortfalls. Typically, an annual inflation rate of 2-3% is a reasonable assumption, but keep an eye on economic trends that might impact this figure.

Additionally, consider potential changes in healthcare expenses.

As we age, our medical needs tend to increase, and healthcare costs can be substantial. Evaluate your current health insurance coverage, and research Medicare options or any supplementary insurance you might require in the future.

Setting Specific Goals

Interestingly enough, With a clearer picture of your financial needs, it's time to set specific, measurable goals.

Use the SMART goals framework as your guide: Specific, Measurable, Achievable, Relevant, and Time-bound.

1.

Specific: Your goals should be precise and unambiguous. Rather than saying, "I want enough money to retire," specify an exact figure or level of income required annually during retirement.

2.

Measurable: Ensure your goals have a clear metric for measuring progress. This could be the amount saved in a retirement account, the number of income-producing investments, or the percentage of expenses covered by passive income.

I've seen this happen before: 3.

Achievable: Set goals that are realistic given your current financial situation. It's important to stretch yourself, but goals should remain within reach to prevent discouragement.

4. **Relevant**: Align each goal with your overarching retirement vision. Relevance ensures that each milestone contributes meaningfully toward fulfilling your desired lifestyle.

5.

Time-bound: Assign a deadline to each goal. Whether it's a specific date or an age milestone, having a timeframe will instigate a greater sense of urgency and accountability.

Prioritizing Goals

Not all goals carry the same weight or urgency. Once you have a list of specific goals, the next task is to prioritize them.

Consider the order of importance based on your unique circumstances and desires. Essential expenses such as housing and healthcare might top the list, while discretionary spending for travel or hobbies might come later. This hierarchy helps allocate your resources wisely.

Aligning Goals with Available Resources

In real life, Setting realistic retirement goals also involves aligning them with your available resources. Conduct a thorough assessment of your current financial status, including savings, investments, income sources, and liabilities.

Identify potential gaps and surpluses. This analysis will help you understand the effort required to achieve each goal and whether adjustments are necessary.

For instance, if your analysis reveals that your savings rate is too low to meet future needs, consider strategies to increase contributions.

This might involve reassessing your budget, cutting unnecessary expenses, or seeking additional income streams. Alternatively, re-evaluate whether your goals are too ambitious and require scaling down.

Creating a Flexible and Adaptive Plan

Interestingly enough, The only certainty about the future is its inherent uncertainty. As such, while setting retirement goals, it's critical to also prepare for change.

Flexibility and adaptability are key components of realistic planning. Life circumstances can alter unexpectedly due to health issues, market conditions, or personal desires shifting over time.

To accommodate this, regularly revisit and revise your goals.

An annual or bi-annual review of your retirement plan allows for timely adjustments. This practice not only provides peace of mind but also enables you to leverage unforeseen opportunities or mitigate risks.

In conclusion, setting realistic retirement goals is both an art and a science. It requires honest self-assessment, meticulous planning, and the flexibility to adapt as circumstances evolve. By defining clear and attainable goals, you lay the foundation for a retirement that's not only secure but also deeply fulfilling.

In the next chapter, we will explore strategies to maximize savings and investments to reach these carefully crafted goals. Until then, take time to reflect on your vision for retirement and the steps needed to transform that vision into reality. Preparing today sets the stage for a tomorrow where retirement is not the conclusion of a career, but the commencement of an enriching new chapter.

Chapter 3: Simplifying Your Finances: A Minimalist Approach

Retirement marks a significant transition from earning a regular income to living primarily on savings and investments. This shift can bring both excitement and anxiety.

One of the most effective strategies to alleviate financial stress in retirement is adopting a minimalist approach to your finances. A minimalist approach doesn't mean cutting out everything you enjoy or living an exceedingly frugal life; instead, it's about focusing on what's truly important, eliminating what's not, and managing your resources in a way that enhances the quality of your life. By simplifying your finances, you can reduce complexity, save time, and enhance your peace of mind.

Understanding Financial Minimalism

At its core, financial minimalism is about clarity and intentionality. It involves understanding where your money comes from, where it goes, and how it can be managed with as little complication as possible.

Many people enter retirement carrying the financial habits and complexities accumulated during their working years. Bank accounts, investments, subscriptions, and insurance policies can all become tangled threads in the financial tapestry of life. The goal here is to weave these threads into a coherent and manageable fabric that supports your lifestyle in retirement.

Streamlining Your Accounts

The first step in simplifying your finances is consolidating your accounts. Over the years, it's common to open multiple bank accounts and investment funds.

While each one might have served a purpose at the time, managing numerous accounts can become overwhelming in retirement. Begin by evaluating each account – do you still need them all? Consider consolidating your investments into a single brokerage account or rolling over past retirement savings into a single IRA. This not only simplifies management but can also help in understanding the performance of your investments and making necessary adjustments.

Additionally, keep your checking and savings accounts minimalistic.

Ideally, one checking account and one savings account should suffice, unless there's a specific need for separate accounts, such as one dedicated to travel. By keeping the number of accounts manageable, you reduce the administrative burden and focus more on the bigger picture rather than the minutiae.

Pruning Unnecessary Expenses

As part of your transition into a minimalist financial lifestyle, examine your monthly expenses. Subscribe to services and utilities that you use and value, and cut out those that don't add to your quality of life.

The average household subscribes to multiple streaming services, news sites, and various memberships that were perhaps necessary at one time or were signed up for on a whim. Review each subscription and decide if it's worth the cost.

Let's not forget, Take a critical look at your spending patterns.

Track your expenses for a few months to see where your money goes. Are there any patterns of waste or overlooked expenses like dining out or unused gym memberships? By identifying these, you can make informed decisions about which expenses align with your retirement goals and which do not.

Budgeting with Intention

A minimalist financial approach also involves setting up a simplified, intentional budget. Traditional budgets can be detailed and overwhelming, but a minimalist budget focuses on broader categories rather than minute details.

Divide your expenses into a few essential categories such as housing, bills and utilities, groceries, healthcare, leisure, and savings. Set reasonable amounts that reflect your retirement lifestyle for each category, and track them monthly.

By reducing the number of budget categories, you have clear guidelines to follow without feeling constrained by too many rules.

This helps in understanding and controlling your expenses without the need for an elaborate spreadsheet that accounts for every individual expense.

Embracing Automation

Technology can be your ally in simplifying financial management. Automate bill payments and savings wherever possible.

Automation reduces the risk of late fees, ensures you're saving consistently, and frees up mental space that was previously occupied by remembering due dates. Many financial platforms offer services to automate these processes, providing reminders, notifications, and easy ways to track progress.

Additionally, consider automating your investments.

Many investment platforms offer robo-advisory services that automatically rebalance your portfolio according to your risk profile and financial goals. This hands-off approach can be especially beneficial in retirement, allowing you to benefit from professional management without the constant need for personal oversight.

Decluttering Paperwork

Decades of work and various financial dealings can leave anyone with a mountain of paperwork. Take time to organize and digitalize your financial documents.

Scan important documents like old tax returns, birth certificates, and property deeds, and save them on a secure cloud service. This reduces physical clutter and the risk of misplacing critical paperwork while providing easy access when needed.

As strange as it sounds, Once documents are organized and digitalized, create a minimalist filing system.

Clearly label files if you keep them physically, or use organized folders and clear naming conventions if using digital storage. This not only simplifies tax time or when updating your will, but it also reduces stress when you need to find a specific document quickly.

Focusing on Financial Education

A minimalist approach doesn't imply ignorance or disengagement from your finances; quite the opposite, it's about fostering understanding and control.

Dedicate time to educate yourself on basic financial principles and the specifics related to your retirement assets. Understanding how Social Security works, how to manage withdrawals, and the tax implications of different types of income can empower you to make informed decisions without constant reliance on financial advisors.

Cultivating Mindful Spending

Finally, a minimalist financial life is about mindfulness. Every spending decision should have a purpose and align with your values.

This approach not only helps in managing expenses but also enriches your life by focusing on experiences and items that truly matter to you. Mindful spending allows for better control over impulse purchases and aligns your financial behavior with your long-term goals.

Conclusion

Believe it or not, Simplifying your finances with a minimalist approach is not about living a deprived life but about prioritizing what truly matters. By clearing financial clutter, consolidating accounts, reducing unnecessary expenses, and embracing technology, you create a financial environment that supports a fulfilled, enjoyable retirement.

In simplifying, there lies the power to enjoy your golden years with less stress, fewer worries, and more freedom to pursue what genuinely enriches your life. This chapter is an invitation to evaluate, reshape, and simplify your financial life for a future that is less burdened by complexity and more filled with possibilities.

Chapter 4: Analyzing Your Current Financial Health

Before you can steer your ship toward the tranquil seas of a simplified retirement, you need a thorough understanding of where you're starting from. Analyzing your current financial health is akin to taking your ship into dry dock for a detailed inspection.

This chapter will guide you through assessing your current financial situation, providing you with a clear picture that will serve as the foundation for your retirement planning. While diving into numbers might seem intimidating, keep in mind that the goal is clarity, which will equip you to make informed and confident decisions.

Understanding Your Assets and Liabilities

Interestingly enough, Start by compiling a comprehensive list of your assets. These are the resources you own that hold value. Common assets include:

- **Real Estate**: This includes your home, rental properties, or any land.

Interestingly enough, - **Savings Accounts and Certificates of Deposit**: Money set aside in various savings instruments.

- **Investment Accounts**: Stocks, bonds, mutual funds, and retirement accounts like 401(k)s and IRAs.

- **Valuable Personal Property**: This might include cars, art, jewelry, or high-value collectibles.

Once you've identified your assets, it's time to tackle your liabilities—these are your financial obligations. They include:

It's worth noting that - **Mortgages**: The remaining balance on any property loans.

- **Credit Card Debt**: Outstanding balances that incur high-interest rates.

- **Loans**: This could cover personal loans, student loans, or car loans.

To be honest, - **Any Other Debt**: Include any money owed to others that you are obligated to repay.

Subtracting your liabilities from your assets provides your net worth, a critical number that provides a snapshot of your overall financial health.

Ideally, this number will be positive, and, over time, it should grow as you pay down debt and accumulate more assets.

Evaluating Your Income and Expenses

At first glance, Next, you need a realistic picture of your cash flow. Begin by calculating your total monthly income. Consider all sources, such as:

- **Salary or Wages**: After-tax income you bring home.

It's worth noting that - **Pensions or Annuities**: Regular payments you might be receiving.

- **Investment Income**: Dividends, interest, or rental earnings.

- **Miscellaneous Income**: Include anything extra, like a side hustle or freelance work.

Now list your expenses, categorizing them into fixed and variable costs:

Believe it or not, - **Fixed Expenses**: These are regular and predictable costs, like mortgage payments, insurance, and utility bills.

- **Variable Expenses**: These can fluctuate monthly and include groceries, entertainment, and dining out.

Let's not forget, Track this meticulously for a few months to identify spending patterns.

There are many tools available, from budgeting apps to simple spreadsheets, to help you keep track.

Understanding your income and expenses will help you recognize areas where you might cut back, which can further increase your capacity to save and invest for retirement.

Assessing Savings and Investment Behavior

Let's not forget, Take a hard look at your savings habits.

What percentage of your income do you consistently save? Are you adequately padding your emergency fund? A general rule is to have three to six months' worth of living expenses saved for emergencies—a safety net that prevents you from dipping into retirement savings or accruing debt if unexpected expenses arise.

Furthermore, analyze your investments. Evaluate your current investment strategy, ensuring it aligns with your retirement goals.

Consider diversification—spreading your investments across different assets to mitigate risk. Are you contributing enough to your retirement accounts, and are you making the most of employer matching if available?.

If you find this area confusing, don't hesitate to consult a financial advisor.

They can help develop a strategy tailored to your risk tolerance and retirement timeline.

Reviewing Insurance Coverage

An often-overlooked aspect of financial health is adequate insurance coverage. Insurance is a crucial component in protecting your assets and income. Consider the following:

- **Health Insurance**: Ensure you have coverage that suits your needs, protecting you from high medical costs.

- **Life Insurance**: Evaluate if your policy adequately replaces income and provides for dependents.

As strange as it sounds, - **Disability Insurance**: This can be vital if you're unable to work due to illness or injury.

- **Property Insurance**: Make sure your home and car have appropriate coverage to avoid potential financial disasters.

It's worth noting that Insurance is a safeguard that ensures your financial plan stays intact in case of unforeseen events.

Regularly review and adjust policies as your life circumstances change.

Identifying Financial Challenges and Opportunities

Now that you've got a handle on your assets, liabilities, income, expenses, savings, and insurance, identify specific challenges and opportunities:

To be honest, - **Debt**: High-interest debt can be a significant drain on your finances.

Develop a plan to reduce or eliminate this as efficiently as possible.

- **Opportunities for Savings**: Look for unnecessary expenditures and areas where you can cut back, funneling the savings toward retirement.

- **Investment Adjustments**: Perhaps there are sectors in which your investments are underperforming compared to market trends—adjust allocations as needed.

Setting Realistic Financial Goals

Interestingly enough, To transition smoothly into retirement, you should set specific, achievable financial goals based on your analysis. These might include:

- Increasing savings rates.

- Aggressively paying off certain debts.

- Increasing contributions to retirement accounts.

- Adjusting investment portfolios to better align with risk tolerance and retirement timeline.

Each goal should be SMART—Specific, Measurable, Achievable, Relevant, and Time-bound. This clarity will guide you in crafting a definitive path toward your retirement objectives.

Conclusion

By meticulously analyzing your current financial health, you lay a solid foundation upon which to build a simplified retirement plan. Equipped with a clear understanding of your financial standing, you can make informed decisions that bring you closer to a secure, uncomplicated retirement.

In the chapters that follow, we'll delve into strategies to enhance your financial standing and explore various paths to achieving a simpler, more secure retirement. Remember, the goal is not just to retire but to do so with peace of mind and simplicity.

Chapter 5: Creating a Simplified Budget for Retirement

Retirement marks the beginning of a new chapter in life, where you have the opportunity to disengage from the rigors of a nine-to-five routine and focus on the activities and passions that bring you fulfillment.

However, transitioning into this phase requires careful financial planning to ensure that your lifestyle remains comfortable and sustainable. Creating a simplified budget for retirement is key to achieving this balance.

Understanding Your Retirement Goals

Before diving into the mechanics of budgeting, it's crucial to have a clear understanding of your retirement goals. Ask yourself what you want your retirement to look like.

Are you planning to travel, pursue a hobby, volunteer, or maybe spend more time with family? Each of these activities comes with its own set of costs. Having a vision of your desired lifestyle provides a foundation for creating a budget that truly supports your dreams.

Evaluating Your Income Sources

Once your goals are set, the next step is to evaluate your income sources.

Unlike regular employment, retirement income often comes from multiple streams such as Social Security benefits, pensions, annuities, and investment returns. Here's a practical approach to mapping out your sources:.

At first glance, 1.

Social Security: Determine when you plan to begin withdrawing Social Security benefits. The age at which you start can significantly impact the size of your monthly payments.

2.

Pension Plans: If you have a pension, understand whether it's a fixed payout or subject to changes, and know how often and how much you will receive.

3.

Investment Income: Calculate your expected earnings from stocks, bonds, and other investments. Consult with a financial advisor to ensure these are in line with your risk tolerance.

I've seen this happen before: 4.

Part-Time Work or Business Income: If you plan to supplement your income with part-time work or a side business, factor these into your budget, considering market demand, your skills, and the time you're willing to invest.

Identifying and Categorizing Expenses

Retirement may lower or eliminate some costs, such as commuting expenses, but others may rise, including healthcare and travel.

Categorizing your expenses helps you understand where your money goes and where adjustments can be made. Consider the following categories:.

I've seen this happen before: - **Housing:** Mortgage, rent, maintenance, and property taxes.

- **Utilities:** Electricity, water, internet, and phone services.

- **Healthcare:** Insurance premiums, medications, and out-of-pocket medical expenses.

Let's not forget, - **Transportation:** Car payments, fuel, public transportation, or new vehicle savings.

- **Food and Groceries:** Groceries, dining out, and entertainment meals.

- **Entertainment and Leisure:** Travel, hobbies, subscriptions, and memberships.

Let's not forget, - **Miscellaneous:** Clothing, gifts, donations, and unexpected expenses.

Setting Priorities and Making Adjustments

With your expenses clearly listed, the next step is prioritizing which ones are essential and which are discretionary.

Essential expenses, such as housing and healthcare, are non-negotiable and should be covered first. For discretionary expenses, such as dining out or luxury purchases, consider setting limits to ensure they don't derail your budget.

Interestingly enough, It is equally important to anticipate inflation and healthcare cost increases. A good rule of thumb is to incorporate an annual increase of 3% into your budget to account for inflation.

For healthcare, expect a slightly higher rate. These allowances ensure you don't find yourself with a shortfall in the years to come.

Utilizing Budgeting Tools

Creating and maintaining a simplified budget is easier with the right tools.

Today's technology offers a variety of software and apps specifically geared towards retirement planning:.

- **Mint:** Tracks and categorizes spending automatically, providing an overall picture of your financial health.

- **Personal Capital:** A more investment-focused tool that also allows for budgeting.

- **You Need a Budget (YNAB):** Encourages proactive budgeting by teaching you to allocate every dollar.

These tools can provide reminders, alerts, and easy-to-read graphs and charts to help you visualize your progress toward meeting financial goals.

Planning for the Unexpected

One of the best defenses against financial instability in retirement is an emergency fund.

Ideally, this fund should cover three to six months of living expenses. Such a cushion serves as a safety net against unexpected costs like major home repairs or emergency medical care without disrupting your overall budget.

Regular Review and Adjustment

Finally, remember that a budget is not a set-it-and-forget-it tool. Economic conditions, personal needs, and desires change over time.

Regularly reviewing your budget—quarterly, semi-annually, or annually—ensures it remains aligned with your financial situation and retirement goals. During these reviews, assess whether you can increase savings in certain areas or need to adjust your spending habits.

Budgeting for retirement doesn't have to be a complex or daunting task.

By understanding your income sources, categorizing expenses, setting priorities, utilizing modern tools, and planning for the unexpected, you set the foundation for a financially secure and fulfilling retirement. A simplified, focused approach is your best bet for ensuring that your golden years are not overshadowed by financial worry but illuminated by the freedom to enjoy each new day.

Chapter 6: The Power of Compounding: Building Wealth Over Time

In the realm of financial planning and retirement security, few concepts are as profound—and perhaps as misunderstood—as the power of compounding.

The famous physicist Albert Einstein is often credited with calling compound interest "the eighth wonder of the world," suggesting that those who understand it, earn it, and those who don't, pay it. In this chapter, we will explore how you can harness this powerful financial force to build wealth over time for a simpler, stress-free retirement.

At its core, compounding is the process by which an asset's earnings—whether from interest or capital gains—are reinvested to generate additional earnings over time.

This mechanism creates a snowball effect: your original investments earn returns, and those returns then earn more returns, and so on. The beauty of compounding lies in its exponential nature, where the longer your money is invested, the more it grows, often in surprising ways.

As strange as it sounds, To illustrate the concept, imagine planting a tree. Initially, it is just a seedling requiring care and nurturing, but as it grows, it starts producing fruit.

In the financial world, these fruits are the interest or returns you earn. With each passing season, the tree becomes more robust, yielding more fruit and seeds, which in turn are reinvested to grow even more trees. Similarly, compounding works best when given time to grow and develop into a substantial wealth generator.

Understanding Compounding: The Basics

First, let's break down how compounding works with a straightforward example. Suppose you invest $1,000 in a savings account with an annual interest rate of 5%. At the end of the first year, you earn $50 in interest. If you reinvest that $50, your investment grows to $1,050.

In the second year, the 5% interest rate applies to the new total, leading to an interest earning of $52. 50 for the second year, making your new balance $1,102. 50. As you can see, each year, the amount of interest earned grows slightly, due to the higher principal as a result of reinvesting previous earnings.

The Time Factor

Time is a pivotal element in the compounding equation. The earlier you start investing, the more time your money has to grow. An example often used in financial circles is that of two investors, Alice and Bob.

Alice starts investing $200 a month at age 25 and stops at age 35, having a total of $24,000 in contributions. Bob begins investing the same amount but starts at age 35 and continues until he turns 65, contributing a total of $72,000 over 30 years. Assuming a 7% annual return, who ends up with more money at age 65?.

Surprisingly, Alice's account balance is significantly larger than Bob's, despite her smaller total contributions.

This discrepancy is due to Alice allowing her investments to compound over a longer period. Thus, time is a powerful ally when it comes to compounding, emphasizing the importance of starting early.

In real life, ### Consistency and Patience: The Keys to Compounding

While starting early is crucial, the consistency of your investment behavior also plays a vital role in maximizing compounding power.

Regular, disciplined contributions—even if they're modest—add up over time. This approach helps mitigate market volatility by adopting a dollar-cost averaging strategy, in which investments are spread out over regular intervals, buying more shares when prices are low and fewer when they are high.

Compounding also teaches the importance of patience. In the early stages of investing, it might seem like progress is slow. However, maintaining a long-term perspective is key.

As evidenced in the Rule of 72—a quick formula to estimate how long it will take for an investment to double at a given annual interest rate—patience can yield impressive results. Divide 72 by your expected annual rate, and you'll see how many years are needed to double your investment. For example, with a 6% rate, your investment will double in about 12 years.

The Role of Reinvestment

Reinvestment amplifies the benefits of compounding.

Whether through dividends, interest, or capital gains distributions, reinvesting these returns rather than cashing them out allows your wealth to grow exponentially. Many financial products, like mutual funds or dividend reinvestment plans, offer automatic reinvestment options, simplifying the process and ensuring you fully capitalize on compounding.

Avoiding the Pitfalls

While compounding can significantly boost your financial wellness, it's important to be wary of potential pitfalls. High-interest debt, for example, works against your financial growth through negative compounding.

Interest on loans like credit card balances can compound rapidly, leading to ballooning debt and financial strain. Minimizing high-interest debt should be a priority in your financial plan to avoid this detrimental form of compounding.

The Tax Implication

Taxes are another factor to consider in compounding. Tax-efficient investment vehicles like Individual Retirement Accounts (IRAs) or 401(k)s can protect your earnings from immediate taxation, allowing your contributions to grow unhindered—a clear advantage for compounding.

Traditional IRAs provide tax-deferred growth, meaning you pay taxes upon withdrawal during retirement, potentially in a lower tax bracket. Conversely, Roth IRAs offer tax-free growth, as contributions are made with after-tax dollars. Both serve as effective tools for maximizing compounding benefits.

Conclusion: Turning Knowledge into Action

The power of compounding is one of the fundamental principles of wealth building. Understanding and harnessing this principle can set you on the path to a secure financial future and a simplified retirement.

Start early, be consistent, reinvest your earnings, and always keep a long-term perspective. Remember, compounding is a marathon, not a sprint—it rewards patience, discipline, and time.

Ultimately, embracing the power of compounding means making informed, diligent financial choices today in order to enjoy the fruits of your efforts tomorrow.

From ensuring you choose the right investment vehicles to managing debt wisely, your actions can significantly impact your retirement readiness. By integrating the principles of compounding into your financial strategy, you are not just saving money, but you are allowing your money to work effectively, building wealth steadily over time—a truly powerful way to achieve a simpler, stress-free retirement.

Chapter 7: Smart Saving Strategies for Everyone

In today's fast-paced world, retirement often feels like a distant mirage hovering just beyond our reach. As we juggle daily expenses and unforeseen financial commitments, the prospect of setting aside money for retirement can seem daunting.

Yet, smart saving strategies can offer a tangible path towards a secure financial future for everyone, regardless of current income level or financial literacy. Let's explore some practical steps to simplify saving, ensuring a more robust retirement plan without the complexity that tiptoes around typical financial advice.

Understand Your Financial Picture

In real life, The first step to effective saving is understanding the full landscape of your finances. Start by mapping out all sources of income. Include salaries, part-time jobs, rental income, and even passive income sources like dividends or interest from investments.

Simultaneously, catalog all your expenses, from major bills like rent or mortgage to the daily cup of coffee or streaming subscriptions. If you're tech-savvy, consider using budgeting apps that automatically tabulate this data and provide clear summaries. Having a clear, realistic picture is critical; it provides the foundation upon which all further strategies will be built.

Create a Personal Saving Goal

Once you have a clear understanding of your financial status, the next step is setting a saving goal. Goals provide direction and motivation.

Whether it's buying a dream home, funding children's education, or ensuring financial independence in retirement, a clearly defined goal is your North Star. Assigning a specific number to this goal—like saving $500,000 for retirement or $30,000 for a home down payment—adds an element of accountability and helps in tracking progress.

Employ the "Pay Yourself First" Strategy

This classic strategy works wonders for ensuring savings don't become an afterthought. Before paying bills or spending on discretionary items, allocate a portion of your income directly to savings.

Automate this transfer if possible. If you're uncertain how much to start with, begin small. Even setting aside 5% of your monthly earnings can create habit momentum, which can be increased as you become more comfortable.

Leverage Retirement Accounts

Let's not forget, One of the smartest ways to save for retirement is leveraging retirement accounts like 401(k)s and IRAs. Not only do these accounts provide tax advantages, but many employers offer matching contributions, effectively giving you free money.

Always contribute enough to meet your employer's match, if available. Understand the contribution limits and tax implications of your chosen accounts and adjust your contributions accordingly. Early and consistent contributions, even if modest, can yield substantial benefits through compound interest over the years.

Embrace Low-Cost Investments

While saving accounts are safe, they provide little in the way of growth. Instead, consider low-cost investments for higher returns. Mutual funds, index funds, and ETFs are excellent choices.

They diversify investments across various companies, reducing individual risk. Ensure you understand the fee structure and historical performance of any fund before investing. Dollar-cost averaging—investing small amounts regularly rather than in lump sums—can further mitigate risk, taking advantage of market fluctuations over time.

Reduce Unnecessary Expenses

We often overlook the impact of small, recurring expenses. Examine recurring expenses such as subscriptions, eating out, or luxury services.

Cutting back doesn't mean eliminating pleasures entirely; it merely involves prioritizing what truly adds value to your life. Batch-cooking meals, reconsidering that gym membership, or opting for a generic instead of brand-name products can result in significant savings over time. Direct these saved funds into your chosen savings strategy.

Build an Emergency Fund

To be honest, Before intensifying other long-term savings, ensure you have an emergency fund in place. This fund acts as your financial safety net, covering unexpected expenses like medical emergencies, sudden job loss, or urgent home repairs.

Aim to have three to six months' worth of living expenses saved. Store this fund in a liquid account, ensuring easy access when emergencies arise. Once the emergency fund is in place, focus on other saving goals with peace of mind.

Harness the Power of Side Hustles

In the digital age, additional income streams are more accessible than ever. Capitalize on skills or hobbies through freelance platforms, part-time gigs, or selling handmade crafts online.

Allocate earnings from side hustles directly to savings or investments, accelerating progress towards your financial goals. Ensure any side job aligns with your lifestyle and doesn't lead to burnout, as balance is critical for long-term sustainability.

Stay Informed and Adjust

Economic landscapes and personal circumstances regularly evolve, making it important to routinely review and adjust your saving strategies. Stay informed on financial news, tax laws, and market trends that might affect your savings.

Adjust your strategies if you receive a raise at work, face new financial obligations, or encounter a lifestyle change. Flexibility allows you to maintain control over your financial destiny, adapting as needed to stay on course.

Educate and Involve Your Family

Smart saving isn't a solo endeavor. Involving family members aligns the household towards unified financial goals.

Encourage open discussions about budgeting, expenses, and savings. Instilling in children a sense of fiscal responsibility sets foundational habits for their future. This comprehensive approach creates a support system, fostering an environment where saving becomes a shared commitment, not a singular task.

Conclusion

Smart saving strategies are within reach for everyone and, more importantly, don't require complex financial maneuvers to be effective. Start simple, with clear goals, and gradually build as comfort and confidence in saving grow.

Tools like retirement accounts, low-cost investments, and emergency funds form a foundation for security, while reducing excess expenses and developing supplemental income streams accelerate progress. Practiced consistently, these strategies ensure that the seemingly elusive goal of a comfortable, well-funded retirement becomes a reality, ready to be enjoyed with peace of mind and financial independence.

Chapter 8: Investing Made Easy: Simplifying Your Portfolio

Investing can often feel like venturing into a labyrinth of ticker symbols, market trends, and complex financial jargon—a world seemingly designed to perplex anyone who doesn't speak the language of Wall Street.

However, if you're yearning for a simple, effective approach to ensure a secure retirement, understand that complexity is not a prerequisite for success. This chapter will guide you in distilling the seemingly intricate world of investing into a manageable strategy focused on simplicity, practicality, and peace of mind.

The Importance of Simplicity in Investing

As strange as it sounds, First and foremost, simplicity is key.

In the realm of personal finance, complexity often leads to confusion. By streamlining your investment strategy, you are more likely to stay informed and engaged, make timely decisions, and reduce the anxiety that comes with managing a cluttered financial portfolio.

Simplification in investing is not just about reducing stress. It's also a tactical advantage.

A simplified investment strategy is easier to manage, which can result in better decision-making over the long term. Rather than spreading yourself thin trying to keep up with a plethora of individual stocks, a focused strategy allows you to concentrate on what's truly important—achieving your retirement goals.

Building a Solid Foundation: Understanding Asset Classes

The foundation of any investment strategy is understanding asset classes.

Generally, they are divided into three main categories: equities, fixed income, and cash equivalents. Familiarizing yourself with these will empower you to better assess risk and reward, ensuring you align with your retirement objectives.

1. **Equities (Stocks):** These represent ownership in a company.

Historically, stocks offer higher returns over the long term, aligned well with a retirement timeline. However, they come with higher volatility. Simplicity comes from choosing broad-market index funds or exchange-traded funds (ETFs) that mirror the overall market's performance.

2. **Fixed Income (Bonds):** Bonds are essentially loans you give to governments or corporations, and they pay you interest over time.

They tend to be less volatile than stocks and can offer a steadier stream of income. Consider investing in bond index funds to keep things straightforward.

I've seen this happen before: 3. **Cash Equivalents:** These include money market funds or short-term Treasury bills.

They are the safest but offer the lowest return, often not even outpacing inflation. While it's essential to have some cash equivalents for liquidity, they shouldn't dominate your investment portfolio.

The Role of Diversification

By now, you've likely heard the adage, "Don't put all your eggs in one basket.

" Diversification is a risk management strategy that mixes a variety of investments within a portfolio, reducing exposure to any single asset or risk. When simplifying your portfolio, the aim is not to eliminate diversification but to streamline how you achieve it.

Interestingly enough, How do you simplify diversification? Use broadly diversified index funds or ETFs.

These instruments offer inherent diversification by pooling together a wide array of assets within one investment. With them, instead of choosing individual stocks or bonds, you're effectively investing in a little piece of a large market segment, which minimizes company-specific risk and sharpens your focus.

Asset Allocation Made Simple

Simplicity in investing also hinges on a clear asset allocation strategy.

Asset allocation refers to how you divide your investments among different asset classes—equities, fixed income, and cash equivalents. The aim is to align your allocation with your goals, time horizon, and risk tolerance.

Interestingly enough, An often-cited rule of thumb is the 'Rule of 100.

' Subtract your age from 100, and the result is the percentage of your portfolio that should be allocated to equities. For example, if you're 60, you might consider placing 40% of your portfolio in stocks and the remaining 60% in bonds and cash equivalents.

While such rules offer simple guidelines, they should not replace personalized insight and consideration.

Online calculators and financial advisors can further simplify this process, providing tailored asset allocation based on individual circumstances and preferences.

Rebalancing: A Simple Maintenance Task

Interestingly enough, Once your allocations are in place, maintaining that balance is crucial. Through rebalancing, you return your portfolio to its intended allocation, usually annually.

This might mean selling assets that have grown beyond their target and buying those that have shrunk. Rebalancing keeps your risk levels in check, ensuring they remain aligned with your retirement plan.

Automating this process can further simplify it.

Many brokerage accounts offer automatic rebalancing, so consider this option to keep your portfolio on track with minimal hands-on effort.

Staying the Course: Patience and Discipline

Market volatility often deters investors from seeing through their strategies, with the tendency to react hastily proving quite detrimental.

The simplified investor appreciates that ups and downs are a natural rhythm of the markets and maintains composure, avoiding impulsive decisions that disrupt long-term goals.

Stick to the plan you've put in place. This requires discipline and a long-term perspective.

Understand that investing is not about timing the market but rather the time spent in the market. A steady, consistent approach usually proves more fruitful and stressful than reacting to every market tremor.

Leveraging Technology

To be honest, In our digital age, technology stands as an ally in simplifying investment management.

Robo-advisors can create and manage a diversified portfolio according to your risk tolerance and goals, often at a lower fee than traditional financial advisors. Robo-advisors provide an excellent hands-off solution to managing your investments, keeping things uncomplicated.

Further, mobile apps with user-friendly interfaces provide real-time insights and updates, allowing you to monitor the performance of your investments effortlessly.

This accessibility translates into better engagement and understanding of your financial position.

Final Thoughts

Believe it or not, Simplifying your portfolio does not mean limiting your opportunities. On the contrary, it focuses your efforts on the most impactful actions, aligning them with your retirement goals.

The beauty of a simplified strategy is that it's easier to understand, manage, and adjust as your needs evolve. Embrace simplicity, and you may find more than just financial return; you may discover a more secure, less stressful path to a fulfilling retirement.

Stay informed, remain disciplined, and allow simplicity to be your guiding principle as you navigate your investment journey.

In doing so, you'll be better equipped to handle the complexities of financial markets and better poised to achieve the financial independence you seek for your golden years.

Chapter 9: Minimizing Debt: Strategies for a Stress-Free Retirement

Retirement should be a time of fulfillment and relaxation, not one burdened by financial stress. Yet, for many, debt poses a significant threat to enjoying the golden years.

Traditionally, retirement was seen as a time to transition from earning an income to living off saved resources. However, lingering debts can disrupt this transition, causing anxiety and strain. In this chapter, we will explore practical strategies to minimize debt, paving the way for a more peaceful retirement.

Evaluate Your Debt Situation

Interestingly enough, Begin by gaining a clear understanding of your current debt situation. This involves listing all outstanding liabilities, such as mortgages, credit card balances, personal loans, and any other financial obligations.

Assess the interest rates, monthly payments, and terms associated with each. This initial step might be daunting, but it's crucial for forming an effective strategy.

Once you have a comprehensive view, categorize your debts into 'good' and 'bad' debt. 'Good' debt typically involves borrowing for investments that may increase in value, such as your mortgage.

'Bad' debt usually comes from borrowing for depreciating assets or consumption purposes, such as credit card debt. Your focus should be eliminating or reducing the 'bad' debt first due to its high-interest rates and lack of long-term value.

Create a Repayment Plan

Believe it or not, With a detailed understanding of your debts, the next step is to create a structured repayment plan.

There are several approaches to consider, two of the most popular being the debt snowball and debt avalanche methods.

The debt snowball method prioritizes paying off the smallest debts first while making minimum payments on larger debts.

This method can provide psychological wins as smaller debts disappear, motivating you through visual and emotional reinforcement.

Alternatively, the debt avalanche method focuses on debts with the highest interest rates.

Over the long term, this approach is often more cost-effective as it reduces the total interest paid.

As strange as it sounds, Choose the method that aligns best with your financial situation and personal motivation.

Commit to making extra payments whenever possible, perhaps by channeling any windfalls, such as tax refunds or bonuses, directly into debt reduction.

Cut Down on Spending

Reducing debt not only involves repaying what's owed but also requires controlling further borrowing. A crucial aspect is cutting unnecessary spending.

Begin by creating a budget that accounts for all your current expenses. Assess your spending habits and identify areas where you can cut back.

As strange as it sounds, Consider downsizing your home if feasible, as this could significantly cut housing expenses. Embrace a simpler lifestyle where luxuries are occasional treats rather than regular expenses.

Evaluate recurring monthly costs such as subscriptions, dining out, and impulse purchases. This exercise isn't about deprivation, but rather aligning your spending with your retirement goals.

Increase Income

Boosting your income is another effective way to tackle debt more aggressively.

If you are still working, consider negotiating for a raise or taking on part-time work or freelancing opportunities that align with your skills and interests. Even in retirement, many find rewarding activities that generate income while ensuring they remain active and engaged.

Let's not forget, Another option is to tap into passive income streams.

Consider renting out a room or property on platforms like Airbnb, or invest in dividend-paying stocks. However, approach investments cautiously and consider consulting a financial advisor to mitigate risks.

Refinancing and Consolidation

Refinancing existing loans at a lower interest rate can reduce monthly payments and total interest over time.

This is particularly relevant for mortgages, where even a small rate drop can result in significant savings.

Many people don't realize this, but Debt consolidation is another strategy worth exploring.

By combining multiple debts into a single loan, usually with a lower overall interest rate, you simplify your repayment process. This approach is especially beneficial for managing various high-interest debts, like credit card balances.

Avoid New Debt

Disciplined financial habits are key to avoiding new debt as you approach or enjoy retirement.

Always weigh the necessity of any new financial commitment, considering both immediate needs and long-term implications. Keep credit card use in check, paying off the balance in full each month if possible to avoid interest charges.

Consider embracing a cash-only habit, forcing you to live within your means.

When it comes to financing larger purchases, prioritize saving up rather than borrowing. This habit can prevent future debt accumulation, granting peace of mind.

Utilize Professional Help

If managing debt becomes overwhelming, don't hesitate to seek professional advice.

Certified financial planners can provide bespoke strategies tailored to your circumstances, helping you navigate complex financial waters. Similarly, credit counselors can assist with budget creation and debt management plans, potentially cutting interest rates or waiving fees through negotiations with creditors.

Conclusion

Minimizing debt is integral to achieving a stress-free retirement. While the journey to address financial obligations can be challenging, the benefits far outweigh the difficulties.

By implementing these strategies, you can transition into retirement with a solid, stable financial footing, ready to enjoy the fruits of your labor without the shadow of debt. Remember, financial freedom isn't merely about the absence of debt – it's about the presence of choice and the security to live your life's next chapter on your own terms.

Chapter 10: Understanding Social Security and Medicare

Navigating the landscape of retirement can be daunting, but two key components that stand solid amidst the complexity are Social Security and Medicare.

These government programs form the backbone of retirement planning for many Americans, ensuring a degree of financial stability and access to healthcare. This chapter aims to dissect these programs, exploring their benefits, requirements, and how best to leverage them to secure a simple, yet stable future.

Understanding Social Security

At first glance, Social Security, established in 1935, is a federal program providing retirement, disability, and survivor benefits.

Funded through payroll taxes under the Federal Insurance Contributions Act (FICA), Social Security serves as a critical income source for retirees. Understanding how it works is crucial for strategic retirement planning.

To qualify for Social Security benefits, you typically need at least 10 years (or 40 quarters) of work.

The amount you receive depends on your average earnings during your 35 highest-paid working years. The Social Security Administration (SSA) provides statements through their website, allowing you to track estimated benefits.

One of the pivotal decisions regarding Social Security is determining when to start claiming benefits. You have the option to begin as early as age 62, but doing so reduces your monthly benefits permanently.

Conversely, delaying until age 70 can increase your benefits substantially. The notion of "Full Retirement Age" (FRA)—which ranges from 66 to 67, depending on your birth year—plays a key role in this decision. At FRA, you receive 100% of your calculated benefits, but they increase by approximately 8% each year you delay past that age, up until 70.

A practical approach to deciding when to claim benefits involves considering your financial needs, life expectancy, and overall retirement goals.

It's beneficial to plot out potential scenarios and remember that Social Security is structured to be actuarially fair, meaning that, on average, total lifetime benefits should be similar regardless of when you start receiving them. However, personal circumstances—such as health status, spousal considerations, and financial needs—can markedly influence this choice.

Social Security for Spouses and Survivors

Social Security's provisions for spouses and survivors can also be a vital part of retirement planning. As a spouse, you may be eligible for benefits based on your own work record or that of your partner.

Generally, spousal benefits can go up to 50% of your partner's FRA amount. On the other hand, survivor benefits allow a surviving spouse to receive the deceased spouse's benefit amount, which can be up to 100% of the deceased's benefits.

At first glance, Understanding these benefits can facilitate better strategic planning, especially for couples thinking about retiring together.

If one spouse earned significantly more than the other, optimizing who claims what and when can make a substantial difference in the total Social Security benefits received by the household.

Navigating Medicare

Just as Social Security is integral to financial security post-retirement, Medicare is crucial for healthcare coverage.

Medicare is a federal health insurance program primarily for people aged 65 and older, but it also covers certain younger people with disabilities and those with End-Stage Renal Disease.

Many people don't realize this, but Medicare consists of several parts. Part A covers hospital insurance, which includes inpatient hospital stays, care in a skilled nursing facility, hospice care, and some home health care.

Most people do not pay a premium for Part A if they or their spouse paid Medicare taxes while working. Part B is medical insurance covering outpatient care, preventive services, ambulance services, and mental health care, among other things. While Part A is often premium-free, Part B requires a monthly premium, which is adjusted based on income.

Part D adds prescription drug coverage and is provided by private insurance companies approved by Medicare.

Enrolling in Part D involves premiums, deductibles, and copayments, necessitating comparison shopping to find a plan that suits your medication needs best.

Additionally, there's Medicare Advantage (also known as Part C), offering an alternative to the original Medicare by bundling Part A, B, and typically D into one plan through a private insurer.

These plans often include extra services like vision, hearing, or dental. However, provider networks can be more limited, so careful scrutiny of plan details is needed.

Enrollment and Strategic Planning

To avoid penalties, it's important to enroll in Medicare Part A and Part B during your initial enrollment period, which lasts seven months and begins three months before you turn 65.

If you are still working and have employer coverage, you may delay Part B without penalty, but careful timing is essential.

Choosing the right Medicare plan can be overwhelming, given the myriad of options. Consider your current health needs, any ongoing treatments, and how these might change with age.

Tools like the Medicare Plan Finder can assist in identifying plans that balance costs and coverage. Importantly, review your plan annually during the open enrollment period, as health needs and plans themselves can change.

Conclusion

Understanding Social Security and Medicare is crucial to simplifying your retirement transition and securing your future. These programs, when applied strategically, offer significant security and peace of mind.

By familiarizing yourself with the particulars of Social Security benefits and wisely choosing among Medicare plans, you can make informed decisions that best suit your financial situation, health needs, and life goals. As complex as they may appear initially, these systems are designed to support you—ensuring that your retirement isn't just about surviving, but thriving.

Chapter 11: Affordable Healthcare in Retirement

Retirement is often seen as a golden period—a time when you finally get to enjoy the fruits of your hard-earned labor.

However, one of the foremost concerns for retirees is the cost of healthcare, a financial factor that can significantly impact the quality of these years. In this chapter, we delve into practical strategies for securing affordable healthcare during retirement, ensuring you can enjoy a healthy, financially stable future.

Understanding Healthcare Needs in Retirement

Believe it or not, Before diving into solutions, it's essential to understand the healthcare landscape you will face in retirement.

Medical needs typically increase with age, and while Medicare provides a safety net, it does not cover all expenses. Understanding the gaps in coverage and anticipating possible healthcare needs is the first step in managing costs effectively.

Medicare: The Healthcare Cornerstone

Medicare is the primary source of health coverage for most Americans aged 65 and older. It comprises different parts, each designed to cover specific services:

To be honest, - **Medicare Part A** covers inpatient hospital care, skilled nursing facility care, hospice, and some home health care.

Most people do not pay a premium for Part A if they or their spouse paid Medicare taxes for a certain period.

- **Medicare Part B** covers outpatient care, doctor's services, preventive services, and some home health care.

This part requires a monthly premium, which is adjusted based on income.

- **Medicare Part C**, or Medicare Advantage, provides an alternative to traditional Medicare.

These plans are offered by private companies approved by Medicare and bundle Parts A and B, often with additional benefits like vision or dental care.

It's worth noting that - **Medicare Part D** covers prescription drugs and is also provided through private plans.

Each Part D plan is different, and costs can vary significantly.

Medicare serves as a crucial baseline, but it's important to remember it won't cover all of your healthcare expenses.

For instance, long-term care services, most dental and eye care, and hearing aids are typically not covered.

Filling the Gaps: Medigap and Supplemental Insurance

Many people don't realize this, but To bridge the coverage gaps left by Medicare, many retirees opt for Medigap, also known as Medicare Supplement Insurance.

Medigap policies, offered by private companies, help pay some of the healthcare costs that Medicare doesn't, such as copayments, coinsurance, and deductibles.

When choosing a Medigap plan, consider the following:

- **Plan Standardization**: Medigap plans are standardized, meaning the benefits are the same regardless of which insurance company you choose.

The primary differences will be in price and potentially service quality.

To be honest, - **Enrollment Period**: The best time to buy a Medigap policy is during your six-month Medigap open enrollment period.

During this time, you can buy any policy sold in your state without the risk of being denied coverage or charged higher premiums due to health issues.

Prescription Drug Costs: Strategies to Save

Prescription drugs can be a significant expense, but there are ways to manage these costs:

As strange as it sounds, - **Review Your Plan Annually**: Medicare Part D plans can change their premiums and covered medications each year.

Reviewing your plan annually during the open enrollment period ensures it still meets your needs and is cost-effective.

- **Generic and Preferred Drug Lists**: Always inquire if there's a generic version of your medication, as these are substantially cheaper than their brand-name counterparts.

Familiarize yourself with your plan's formulary, a list of covered drugs, especially those marked as "preferred," which offer additional savings.

- **Discount Programs**: Numerous pharmacies and insurance companies offer discount programs that are sometimes even more financially favorable than using insurance.

Investigate these offerings in your area.

Long-Term Care: Planning Ahead

One of the major healthcare expenses in retirement is long-term care, which includes services like personal care, living assistance, and support for chronic illnesses.

This type of care is not covered under Medicare. Therefore, planning for potential long-term care is essential:.

- **Long-Term Care Insurance**: Purchasing a long-term care insurance policy can be a prudent decision, ideally in your 50s or early 60s when you are still in good health.

These policies help cover the cost of care that isn't covered by health insurance, Medicare, or Medicaid.

In real life, - **Hybrid Policies**: Consider hybrid policies that combine life insurance with long-term care insurance.

These offer the dual benefits of a death benefit along with long-term care coverage. They can be attractive since they provide a level of assurance that you or your heirs will receive some benefit from the policy.

- **Medicaid Planning**: If paying for long-term care insurance isn't feasible, planning to qualify for Medicaid, which covers long-term care in certain eligible cases, might be necessary.

This often involves strategic asset allocation and possibly consulting with a financial planner or attorney specialized in elder law.

Preventive Care: A Cost-Effective Approach

Many people don't realize this, but Preventive healthcare is one of the most cost-effective strategies to maintain your health.

Medicare Part B covers many preventive services with no cost to you, including screenings for heart disease, diabetes, and various cancers. Regular physical exams and engaging in health maintenance behaviors, like exercise and a balanced diet, can prevent or mitigate many health issues, reducing long-term costs.

Community and State Programs

Look into community resources and state programs that offer assistance to retirees.

These programs can include state-specific supplements to Medicare, prescription drug assistance programs, or access to affordable health clinics. Being proactive in seeking these resources can fill in gaps for those living on a fixed income.

Final Thoughts

Affordable healthcare in retirement requires a proactive, informed approach. Leveraging Medicare effectively, supplementing it with appropriate additional insurance, planning for long-term care, and maintaining a preventive health regime can significantly reduce healthcare costs.

Engaging with financial planners or elder care attorneys can provide personalized strategies based on your situation. By taking these steps, you can secure a future where financial concerns do not overshadow the joys of retirement.

Chapter 12: Downsizing: Streamlining Your Lifestyle for the Future

As you stand at the precipice of retirement, one word that might have started echoing in your mind is "simplification. " You've reached a stage in life where complexity often tangles more than it empowers.

Downsizing, when done thoughtfully, can be the key to unraveling these complexities, allowing you to streamline your lifestyle in preparation for the manifold possibilities of your future. This chapter delves into the essentials of downsizing, aiming to provide you with practical insights that will help you transition smoothly into the next chapter of your life.

Understanding Downsizing

As strange as it sounds, Downsizing isn't merely about reducing the number of possessions; it's about curating an environment that supports the life you want to live.

It's an opportunity to shed the surplus, refocus on what truly matters, and prepare for a retirement characterized by freedom rather than encumberment. Often, downsizing is mistakenly feared as a loss, when in reality it is a gain — a gain in clarity, in financial prudence, and in quality of life.

The Motivations Behind Downsizing

Understanding the motivations behind downsizing is crucial. Typically, retirees consider downsizing because maintaining a large home that once accommodated a bustling household no longer suits their needs.

There can also be financial incentives: smaller homes generally come with reduced utility bills, maintenance costs, and property taxes. Beyond finances, retirees often find a smaller space easier to manage physically, which becomes increasingly important as we age.

Believe it or not, Moreover, downsizing aligns with a growing desire for minimalism, a lifestyle choice that champions the idea that less is more.

As you shift focus from accumulation to experience, downsizing can be a liberating move that reorients priorities and maximizes the potential for new adventures and relationships.

The Process of Downsizing

Assessing Your Current Situation: Begin by understanding the size and nature of the home you currently live in.

What are its daily expenses — direct and indirect? Analyze your needs and aims: do you intend to travel, live closer to family, or move to a community conducive to your hobbies and interests?.

At first glance, **Planning Your Space Needs:** Consider the practicalities of your future home.

How much living space do you actually need? What kind of layout will facilitate your lifestyle? Perhaps a single-story home is ideal to reduce the stress of stairs, or maybe an apartment in a retirement community offers social connections along with convenience.

Financial Implications: Calculate the potential savings from reducing home-related expenses.

Equally important is to budget for moving costs and any renovations needed in the new, smaller home to tailor it to your needs. A financial advisor can help you evaluate how these changes might impact your retirement savings and long-term financial health.

Practical Steps for Downsizing

As strange as it sounds, 1. **Start Small:** Decluttering can seem overwhelming, so start small.

Target one room or storage area at a time. Sorting through a single closet will make the whole process feel more manageable.

2.

Categorize and Prioritize: Divide your possessions into categories: keep, donate, sell, or discard. Be honest and mindful — does the item serve a purpose or bring joy? This Marie Kondo-esque approach can significantly reduce what you hold on to without feeling deprived.

3. **Consider Digital Solutions:** Heavy correspondence, photos, and many types of media can be digitized, saving physical space and increasing accessibility.

It's worth noting that 4.

Embrace Technology: Smart home devices can further simplify a retiree's lifestyle, making daily operations easier, from automated lighting to assisted monitoring systems. Leverage technology for sustainability; energy-efficient appliances and smart thermostats can contribute significantly to energy conservation.

5.

Simplify the Move: Engage with moving professionals who understand the needs and sensitivities of retirees. This includes everything from hiring a reputable moving company to obtaining assistance with unpacking and setting up your life in the new space.

6.

Explore Housing Alternatives: Consider various types of housing — from condos to tiny houses, or even shared living arrangements. Many retirees find joy and companionship in co-living situations where they can share upkeep responsibilities and inevitable social interactions.

Interestingly enough, 7. **Evaluate the Emotional Aspects:** Downsizing involves emotional decisions.

It may include leaving a family home filled with memories. Allow yourself the space to grieve these changes and share the experience with family or friends who can support you through the transition.

The Benefits of a Streamlined Lifestyle

The advantages of downsizing endow retirees with enhanced physical maneuverability and fiscal flexibility.

The decrease in home-related labor and costs can free valuable time and financial resources. Moreover, with fewer possessions, the mind is relieved of the clutter that can inhibit focus and relaxation.

Many people don't realize this, but Having a lighter load enables you to embrace what truly enhances your retirement experience, whether that entails travel, hobbies, or simply enjoying a calm, manageable space.

Living more simply often leads to increased mental clarity, reduced stress, and a higher quality of life.

Final Thoughts

Downsizing should be approached not as an act of depriving oneself but as an empowering realignment of life goals and needs.

It provides a foundation for a retirement devoid of complexity and rich with the promise of newfound freedoms and experiences. Transparency in your intentions, a keen awareness of your practical needs, and a healthy acknowledgment of your emotional ties will guide this transition.

Ultimately, downsizing is far more than a physical endeavor; it's a rite of passage into a more intentional, thoughtful existence.

By releasing the physical and emotional burdens of surplus, you prepare yourself to embrace the future with open arms and renewed vigor. This streamlined lifestyle, tailored to your needs and desires, offers the foundation for a fulfilling and secure retirement.

Chapter 13: Embracing Technology for a Simplified Retirement

In the landscape of modern retirement, technology stands as both a challenge and an opportunity.

For those who grew up in a pre-digital age, the rapid advancement can seem daunting. Yet, embracing technology is not merely about keeping up; it's about enhancing the quality of life, staying connected, and securing your future with less complexity.

The first step in embracing technology is adopting a mindset of curiosity rather than resistance. Remember, technology is designed to be intuitive and user-friendly.

The initial hurdle often lies in apprehension, not in complexity. By shifting to a positive perspective, you open yourself up to learning and, ultimately, simplifying your life. Let's explore how technology can transform your retirement in several key areas.

1. Financial Management:

Technology has revolutionized the way we handle money—a boon for retirees seeking simplicity.

With online banking and financial management tools like Mint, Quicken, or Personal Capital, you can effortlessly track your expenditures, manage investments, and plan budgets with a few clicks. These platforms often provide detailed insights into your spending habits and help you identify areas to save.

Embrace online banking to streamline transactions, pay bills, and transfer funds without leaving home.

Most banks offer mobile apps that make it easy to check balances and receive transaction alerts that help prevent fraud. Additionally, video consultations with financial advisors are now common, allowing you to discuss your financial plan from the comfort of your home.

2. Communication and Social Connection:

Retirement does not mean social isolation. In fact, staying connected is crucial for a fulfilling retirement.

Video calling apps like Zoom, Skype, or FaceTime allow you to maintain regular contact with family and friends, regardless of geographic distances. Social media platforms, when used judiciously, can also be a way to stay up-to-date with loved ones and rekindle old friendships.

For the tech-wary, start with simple apps and gradually explore more features.

Many manual guides and free online tutorials simplify learning how to use these tools effectively. Once you've mastered the basics, you'll find it easier to engage in virtual gatherings, join online groups, and participate in forums that match your interests.

3. Health and Well-being:

As you age, maintaining good health becomes crucial, and technology plays a pivotal role here too.

Wearable devices like Fitbit or Apple Watch track your physical activity, monitor heart rates, and even remind you to take medication. They offer an accessible way to maintain an active lifestyle and set fitness goals.

Telehealth services also make healthcare more accessible.

You can consult with healthcare professionals through video chats, which reduces the need for frequent in-person visits. Many health systems offer patient portals, where you can review your medical records, schedule appointments, and even request prescription refills online.

4. Learning and Entertainment:

Retirement is the perfect time to pursue passions or learn new skills.

With platforms like Coursera, Udemy, or MasterClass, you have access to a multitude of online courses worldwide. Whether you've always wanted to learn a new language, delve into photography, or study history, the resources are literally at your fingertips.

For leisurely moments, streaming services, including Netflix, Amazon Prime, and YouTube, provide endless entertainment options.

Podcasts and audiobooks also offer a wealth of information and storytelling that can enrich your downtime or accompany your walks.

5. Home Management:

Smart home technology can alleviate many of the burdens of day-to-day chores, providing safety, convenience, and peace of mind.

Devices like smart thermostats adjust temperatures automatically, enhancing comfort and saving on utility bills. Voice assistants, like Amazon's Alexa or Google Assistant, can manage tasks such as setting reminders, shopping lists, or even controlling other smart devices with simple commands.

Security systems, including smart locks and video doorbells like Ring, enable you to monitor your home remotely, ensuring a sense of security.

These technologies are especially beneficial if traveling often or maintaining multiple residences.

Navigating Privacy and Security Concerns:

One important aspect of integrating technology into your retirement is prioritizing security. Protecting your information in the digital world is paramount, as cyber threats continue to evolve.

Use strong, unique passwords for each account and consider a password manager to keep track of them securely. Enable two-factor authentication where possible for an extra layer of security.

Be cautious about phishing scams, which often target seniors, as they tend to be less familiar with digital nuances.

Verify the legitimacy of emails and websites before sharing personal information. Regularly update your software and devices, as these updates often include critical security patches.

Conclusion:

Technology doesn't have to be a source of anxiety.

Approached with an open mind, it can be a powerful ally in creating a simpler, more connected, and more secure retirement. By slowly integrating various technological tools into your daily life, you stand to gain significant benefits—from managing finances more efficiently to enriching your social and cultural experiences.

In the end, embracing technology isn't about transforming your life overnight.

It's about taking small steps forward, learning at your own pace, and recognizing the potential of these tools to simplify and enhance your retirement. As you become more comfortable, technology becomes a bridge to deeper engagement and a less complicated lifestyle, proving invaluable in this richly rewarding phase of life.

Chapter 14: Alternative Income Streams in Retirement

Retirement is often envisioned as a period of relaxation and enjoyment, where one can finally indulge in hobbies, travel, or spend quality time with loved ones.

While financial planning for retirement typically focuses on savings, pensions, and social security benefits, establishing alternative income streams can offer a crucial buffer and even enrich your retirement experience. This chapter aims to explore several practical avenues for generating income during your retirement, ensuring both financial stability and flexibility.

Embrace the Gig Economy

In real life, The gig economy isn't just for millennials looking for side hustles. It offers retirees a unique opportunity to leverage their skills and experience without the commitments of a full-time job.

Platforms such as Upwork, Fiverr, or TaskRabbit can be excellent for retirees skilled in writing, graphic design, accounting, or even handyman services. These platforms offer the flexibility to set your hours and choose projects that interest you, creating an income stream that can be both rewarding and tailored to your lifestyle.

Moreover, driving for companies like Uber or Lyft, or delivering groceries with Instacart, can be viable options if you enjoy being on the move and interacting with people.

These roles not only provide supplemental income but also keep you socially engaged, a crucial aspect of mental well-being during retirement.

Turn Hobbies into Revenue

It's worth noting that Many retirees find joy in hobbies that can potentially generate income. Whether you enjoy gardening, crafting, painting, or woodworking, there are markets for your products.

Websites like Etsy allow artisans to sell homemade goods, reaching a global audience without the need for physical storefronts. Similarly, gardeners can sell fresh produce or plants at local farmer's markets or through community-supported agriculture (CSA) programs.

If you have a knack for teaching, consider offering classes or workshops.

Many people are eager to learn new skills from experienced practitioners, and online platforms like Teachable or Udemy have made it easier than ever to share your knowledge with others, providing you with an additional income source.

Real Estate Investment

At first glance, Real estate can be an excellent source of steady income if managed wisely.

If you own additional property or have spare space in your primary residence, consider renting it out. Platforms like Airbnb or VRBO allow you to rent on a short-term basis, providing flexibility to use the space yourself or accommodate visiting family and friends.

Another approach is investing in rental properties.

While this requires a more significant initial investment and ongoing management, it can lead to consistent cash flow. You might consider hiring a property management company to handle day-to-day operations, making this income stream largely passive while ensuring your investment is well-maintained.

Dividend Stocks and Interest Income

As strange as it sounds, Investing in dividend-paying stocks or bonds can provide a reliable income stream while allowing your money to continue growing.

These financial instruments pay out a portion of the company's earnings or interests, typically on a quarterly basis, which can be reinvested or used to supplement retirement income.

However, it's crucial to choose your investments wisely.

Diversification is key; consider a mix of high-yield and stable dividend stocks to balance risk and reward. Consulting with a financial advisor can help tailor an investment strategy that aligns with your risk tolerance and financial goals.

Freelancing and Consulting

Interestingly enough, Transitioning from a career to retirement doesn't necessarily mean leaving your professional life behind.

Many retirees find fulfillment and financial benefit in consulting or freelancing in their previous field of work. Offering your expertise on a part-time basis allows you to maintain professional connections and stay intellectually engaged, often at a senior-level pay rate.

Consider reaching out to former colleagues or employers to explore consulting opportunities.

Alternatively, platforms like LinkedIn can help showcase your experience and attract potential clients or freelance gigs. This path not only yields income but provides a sense of continuing purpose and identity post-retirement.

Monetize Your Home

For many retirees, their home is their most valuable asset. Consider strategies to leverage your home for income without selling and relocating.

Home equity conversion through a reverse mortgage can offer a steady income stream, although it's essential to understand the implications on estate planning and future income. Many banks and financial institutions offer workshops and consultations to navigate these options effectively.

Alternatively, you could downsize to a smaller, more manageable property if your current home is larger than needed.

The proceeds from selling your current home can be used to purchase a smaller home, with the remaining balance invested to generate income.

Peer-to-Peer Lending

As strange as it sounds, For those comfortable with technology and looking for a more unconventional investment, peer-to-peer (P2P) lending platforms such as LendingClub or Prosper allow you to lend money directly to individuals or small businesses.

In return, you receive principal and interest payments, creating a potentially high-yield income stream.

This investment carries higher risks, so it should be approached with careful consideration and ideally should not constitute a major portion of your investment portfolio.

Evaluate borrower profiles meticulously and consider spreading smaller amounts across various loans to minimize risk.

Conclusion

By exploring alternative income streams, retirees can ensure greater financial security and maintain a fulfilling, dynamic lifestyle. Each option requires different levels of time, investment, and involvement.

It's essential to assess how these will integrate with your retirement goals, personal interests, and current financial situation. Ultimately, the key is to choose avenues that not only promise financial returns but also enhance quality of life, allowing you to enjoy retirement on your terms.

Chapter 15: Legal Essentials: Wills, Trusts, and Estate Planning

In navigating the retirement landscape, legal preparedness is a cornerstone for ensuring peace of mind and security.

This chapter is dedicated to unraveling the complexities surrounding wills, trusts, and estate planning, equipping you with the knowledge to make informed decisions that uphold your wishes and protect your loved ones.

Understanding the Importance of Estate Planning

Many people don't realize this, but Estate planning is the process of organizing your affairs and distributing your assets effectively upon your death.

It goes beyond mere wealth allocation; it dictates the management of your financial and personal matters in accordance with your values and desires. Without a proper estate plan, the fate of your assets—and by extension, your family's future—could be at the mercy of state laws and courts that may not align with your intentions.

The Will: Your Voice After Death

A will, also known as a last will and testament, is the foundational document of any estate plan.

It specifies how you wish your assets to be distributed, names guardians for minor children, and appoints an executor to manage the distribution process.

Components of a Will:

- **Distribution Instructions:** Clearly outline who receives what, whether it be family members, friends, or charitable organizations.

- **Guardianship:** Nominate individuals to care for your minor children, ensuring their upbringing aligns with your hopes and values.

- **Executor Appointment:** Your executor, often a trusted family member or professional, handles the logistical aspects, from settling debts to distributing assets according to your instructions.

Creating a Will: Best Practices

- **Consult a Professional:** While DIY kits are available, consulting a legal professional ensures your will is compliant with state laws.

- **Clarity and Detail:** Ambiguities lead to disputes. Be explicit in your instructions and use precise language.

- **Regular Updates:** Life changes like births, deaths, and acquisition of assets necessitate updating your will to reflect your current wishes.

Trusts: Flexibility and Control

Many people don’t realize this, but Trusts offer an additional layer of control and can serve purposes that extend beyond the limitations of a will.

They are legal entities that hold assets on behalf of beneficiaries, managed by a trustee you appoint.

Types of Trusts:

In real life, - **Revocable Living Trusts:** Allow the grantor to maintain control over the assets during their lifetime, with the ability to amend or dissolve the trust as circumstances change.

- **Irrevocable Trusts:** Once established, these cannot be easily altered. They are often used for tax advantages and protection from creditors.

- **Special Needs Trusts:** Protect beneficiaries with disabilities, allowing them to receive inheritances without compromising government benefits.

Advantages of Trusts:

- **Avoidance of Probate:** Assets within a trust bypass the often lengthy and costly probate process, facilitating a faster distribution.

To be honest, - **Privacy:** Unlike wills, which are public records, trusts provide privacy by keeping the details out of public view.

- **Control:** Trusts allow you to set conditions and stipulations, such as age or milestone-related disbursements, ensuring that assets are used responsibly.

The Estate Planning Process

Embarking on estate planning requires a methodical approach to encapsulate your life's work and safeguard your interests.

Step 1: Inventory Your Assets

Begin by compiling a comprehensive list covering tangible and intangible assets—real estate, bank accounts, retirement accounts, investments, insurance policies, and personal belongings.

Don't overlook digital assets, such as online accounts and digital currencies.

Step 2: Determine Your Goals

Consider what you hope to achieve with your estate plan.

Identifying primary goals—be it minimizing taxes, protecting heirs, or supporting charities—helps steer the structuring of your plan toward achieving these objectives.

Step 3: Choose Your Tools

Leverage the strengths of wills and trusts by analyzing which is most appropriate for each asset and aspect of your plan.

Employ legal instruments like power of attorney and advance healthcare directives to cover incapacitation scenarios.

Step 4: Execute Legal Documents

With goals and structures defined, work with your attorney to draft and execute legal documents.

Ensure all paperwork reflects current laws and encompasses necessary signatures and notarization.

Step 5: Communicate Your Plan

Inform key parties about your estate plan, including the executor, trustees, and guardians. Discuss their roles and affirm their willingness to uphold your wishes.

Step 6: Review and Revise

Periodically re-assess your estate plan.

Marital status changes, births, deaths, and asset purchases are all triggers for review. Regular updates ensure it remains aligned with your intentions.

Common Pitfalls and How to Avoid Them

Believe it or not, Estate planning missteps can lead to unintended consequences. Here we highlight some common pitfalls and strategies to avoid them:

- **Neglecting Updates:** Failing to revise your plan can render it obsolete. Schedule regular reviews to accommodate life changes.

At first glance, - **Overlooking Digital Assets:** In today's digital era, neglecting online accounts can lead to loss and complexity.

Include login credentials and instructions for digital assets in your estate plan.

- **Ignoring Tax Implications:** Estate taxes can drastically reduce the inheritances left for your beneficiaries.

Consult a tax professional to explore ways to mitigate such liabilities.

- **Incomplete Execution:** Ensure compliance with all legal requirements during document execution to prevent challenges later.

Estate planning might seem daunting, but it is an empowering exercise that secures your legacy and protects your loved ones. By systematically addressing wills, trusts, and other essential elements, you lay the foundation for a financially sound and orderly transfer of assets.

Enlist the aid of professionals, stay informed, and keep communication lines open with those affected by your decisions. Your diligence in this legal journey will cultivate peace of mind today and a lasting impact tomorrow.

Chapter 16: Adapting to Change: Flexibility in the Later Years

As we journey through life, we often envision the later years as a serene and unchanging landscape. The reality, however, is that change is a constant companion, even in retirement.

Embracing this idea can significantly improve your retirement experience, allowing for a fulfilling and adaptive lifestyle. In this chapter, we'll explore practical ways to foster flexibility and resilience in facing the inevitable changes that come with aging.

Understanding the Nature of Change

In real life, First, it's crucial to recognize what kinds of changes can occur in your later years. These can include health fluctuations, shifts in financial stability, evolving social circles, and even housing transitions.

Changes can be anticipated—like downsizing your home—or unexpected, such as a medical diagnosis. Understanding that change is multi-faceted prepares you better for proactive adaptation.

Flexibility doesn't mean being unprepared; rather, it involves anticipating possible changes and having a mindset and plan to adjust accordingly.

By adopting a flexible approach, you invite adaptability into your life, making transitions smoother and less daunting.

Financial Flexibility

At first glance, Financial stability is often the cornerstone of a secure retirement.

However, staying flexible in your financial planning is equally critical. Economic fluctuations, healthcare costs, and unexpected expenses are all realities that require adaptive financial strategies.

1. Diversify Your Income Sources:

Believe it or not, Consider diversifying your income.

This might involve maintaining a part-time job, starting a small business, or generating income from investments. Having multiple streams of income can provide a safety net during economic downturns or unexpected expenses.

2. Contingency Funds:

Interestingly enough, Ensure that you have a robust emergency fund.

This stash should be easily accessible and contain enough to cover several months of living expenses. This buffer not only cushions the blow of sudden financial needs but also grants peace of mind.

3. Revisit and Adjust Budgets:

In real life, Regularly reviewing and adjusting your budget is crucial.

As your priorities and circumstances change, so should your spending plans. Annual or bi-annual budget reviews can help you align your finances with current realities.

Health and Wellness Flexibility

Health is another domain where flexibility is invaluable. As you age, your health needs and capabilities may change, demanding a proactive adaptation approach.

1. Stay Informed and Proactive:

Keeping up with regular health screenings and being informed about your medical conditions allows for timely interventions.

Engage with healthcare professionals and stay updated on health plans and coverage, ensuring that your needs are adequately met.

2. Adapt Your Fitness Routine:

Physical activity is a crucial aspect of maintaining health.

However, your routine might need adjustment as you age. Consult with fitness experts to develop a regime that considers your current abilities and health conditions.

3. Diet and Nutrition Adjustments:

Nutritional needs may change as metabolism slows and health concerns emerge.

Work with a nutritionist to customize your diet, ensuring you get the necessary nutrients without compromising your health.

Social Adaptability

Your social landscape can also shift considerably in your later years.

Friends may move away, loved ones may pass, and interests might evolve. Maintaining a vibrant social life involves being open to these changes.

1. Embrace New Social Opportunities:

Look for community events, classes, or clubs that foster social interaction.

Being part of social groups not only enriches your life with new experiences and friendships but also provides support networks.

2. Leverage Technology:

Technology can bridge the physical gap between you and distant friends or family.

Becoming tech-savvy—even at a basic level—allows you to maintain connections through video calls, social media, and digital correspondence.

3. Volunteer and Give Back:

Consider volunteering.

It offers a sense of purpose and community engagement. By contributing your skills to help others, you strengthen your social connections while enriching the lives of those around you.

Emotional Flexibility

I've seen this happen before: Emotional resilience is often overlooked but remains crucial as you face the inevitable changes in your later years.

1. Practice Mindfulness and Meditation:

Interestingly enough, Incorporating mindfulness or meditation into your daily routine can bolster emotional well-being.

These practices foster a balanced outlook, helping you respond calmly to life's challenges.

2. Seek Emotional Support:

It's worth noting that Never underestimate the value of professional counseling or support groups.

Sharing your experiences with others who understand your situation can alleviate feelings of isolation and stress.

3. Cultivate Positive Mindsets:

Believe it or not, Adopting a positive approach does not mean ignoring life's difficulties; rather, it involves acknowledging challenges while choosing to focus on solutions and gratitudes.

This mindset can enhance emotional flexibility.

Housing and Living Arrangements

It's not uncommon for living arrangements to change as you age.

Whether due to mobility issues, financial considerations, or personal preferences, being prepared for potential housing transitions is wise.

1. Evaluate Current Living Arrangements:

Assess your current home for adaptability as you age.

Are there stairs that might pose difficulties in the future? Is it too large to maintain? Answering these questions can guide necessary adjustments or inspire a move to more suitable housing.

2. Explore Retirement Communities:

Retirement communities offer various levels of care and social engagement options. Exploring these can help you better prepare if a move becomes necessary.

3. Plan for In-home Modifications:

For those wishing to age in place, consider proactive modifications.

Installing grab bars, widening doorways, and other home adjustments can make staying in your home safer and more practical as you age.

Embracing a Flexible Mindset

Ultimately, adapting to change in later years involves embracing a mindset dedicated to flexibility. Strive to remain open to new experiences, learn continuously, and be willing to adjust your expectations and strategies.

By doing so, you pave the way for a dynamic, resilient, and rewarding retirement. Flexibility isn't about predicting the future; it's about equipping yourself with the skills and attitude needed to navigate whatever comes your way.

Chapter 17: Finding Purpose: Staying Engaged and Active

Entering retirement can feel like the dawn of a new era, a time filled with opportunities and freedom.

However, the absence of a structured work routine may also lead to a lack of purpose, unless you actively seek out activities and pursuits that ignite passion and engagement. This chapter delves into practical ways to maintain purpose and stay both mentally and physically active during retirement, so that these years become some of the most fulfilling of your life.

Embrace Lifelong Learning

Let's not forget, One of the greatest gifts of retirement is the freedom to learn without the pressure of deadlines or formal requirements. Lifelong learning is a dynamic way to stay mentally active and engaged.

Community colleges and universities often offer courses tailored for retirees through programs like Osher Lifelong Learning Institutes (OLLI). These courses span an array of interests, from history and literature to gardening and technology.

Online learning platforms like Coursera, edX, and Khan Academy provide access to thousands of courses from top universities globally.

Whether you're looking to dive into a new discipline or refine existing skills, these platforms make education flexible and accessible.

Practical Tip:

Allocate a small educational budget annually.

Subscribing to a few high-quality courses can lead to new hobbies and social opportunities. Treat it like an investment in your cognitive vitality.

Volunteering: A Dual Purpose

Believe it or not, For many, the concept of purpose is indelibly linked to giving back. Volunteering is an excellent way to contribute meaningfully while maintaining a sense of purpose.

Whether it's mentoring, participating in environmental conservation efforts, or assisting in local schools, the options are vast. Websites like VolunteerMatch and local community centers can help match your interests with available opportunities.

Volunteering not only benefits others but also enriches the volunteer. It offers opportunities to make new friends, learn different perspectives, and discover joy in altruism.

Practical Tip:

Start by assessing what causes resonate most with you.

Visit local organizations to see where you can contribute effectively and feel a genuine sense of involvement.

Physical Activity Beyond Exercise

Staying physically active is crucial for health and well-being, adding vitality to your retirement years.

Physical activity, however, does not have to be confined to traditional forms of exercise. Dance classes, yoga, tai chi, hiking, or even gardening can be both fulfilling and excellent for maintaining physical fitness.

Group activities ensure a social component, which is equally beneficial. Senior centers often have a range of classes tailored for different physical abilities and interests.

Practical Tip:

Establish a weekly routine.

Consider joining a social sports league or attend regular community fitness classes. This embeds socializing into your fitness regime, offering dual benefits.

Creative Expressions

Interestingly enough, Retirement is an ideal time to explore your creative side.

Engaging in artistic pursuits like painting, writing, music, or crafting stimulates the brain and provides emotional depth. Creativity is not about producing masterpieces; it's about expressing yourself and enjoying the process.

Consider joining local art clubs or workshops where you can learn new techniques and share your work with others.

Libraries and community centers often host free classes. Remember, the journey is the reward.

Practical Tip:

Commit to one small creative project per month.

Set achievable goals like completing a short story, or creating a set number of art pieces. Revisit these goals to spark continuous motivation.

Building Community

Many people don’t realize this, but Social connections are invaluable.

Building or maintaining a social network can dramatically enhance the quality of retirement. Regular interactions reduce the risk of loneliness and depression, both of which can emerge during this life transition.

Start small by establishing a routine that involves community or peer interaction.

It could be joining book clubs, attending local events, or being part of hobby groups with regular meetings.

Practical Tip:

Host a monthly gathering or event in your home.

It's an excellent way to bring people together. Additionally, consider scheduled social activities like group travel excursions, which combine new experiences with companionship.

Embracing Technology

It’s worth noting that Embracing technology can open new worlds for engagement and interaction.

Social media platforms like Facebook or LinkedIn can be utilized not just for social connections, but also for joining interest groups and staying updated on communities and events.

Genealogy websites like Ancestry.

com connect you to familial roots, offering an exciting journey into your history and purpose. Technology-focused senior centers or tech workshops help build confidence and skills to navigate digital resources effectively.

Practical Tip:

Allocate regular time to explore new technologies and platforms.

Attend workshops or webinars focused on updating digital skills. This not only keeps you engaged but also bridges generation gaps with younger family members and friends.

Travel and Exploration

Interestingly enough, The exploration of new places offers an abundance of experiences that can be both educational and relaxing.

Travel doesn't necessarily require reaching far-flung destinations; it includes visiting local landmarks or exploring history-rich neighborhoods close to home.

Consider volunteer vacations, where you can help communities as you travel, combining altruistic work with the joy of exploration.

This can also provide significant personal growth experiences and story-worthy adventures.

Practical Tip:

Plan seasonal trips, whether small weekend getaways or longer vacations. Keep a travel journal to cherish memories, share insights, and maintain enthusiasm for each adventure.

Conclusion

At first glance, Staying engaged and active in retirement is a choice that requires intention and a proactive approach. By exploring new interests, investing in social relationships, embracing education, and practicing altruism, the possibilities for a purposeful retirement are endless.

Remember, retirement is not about slowing down but shifting gears. Align your activities with your passions, continuously set new goals, and most importantly, embrace this phase as a rich, rewarding chapter of your life.

Chapter 18: Building a Support Network

As you approach retirement, the notion of freedom and leisure often looms invitingly on the horizon. Yet, while the allure of open schedules and the absence of workplace commitments is undeniable, it's important not to overlook the critical role that a well-constructed support network plays in a fulfilling retirement.

A nurturing community can enhance the richness of this life stage, providing emotional support, companionship, and practical assistance. In this chapter, we explore the steps to building and maintaining a robust support system that will serve you throughout your retirement years.

Understanding the Importance of a Support Network

Many people don't realize this, but In its simplest form, a support network is a circle of relationships that provides emotional, social, and practical support when needed. It offers a safety net that allows you to navigate the complexities of personal and health-related challenges with more ease.

As people age, their circles naturally evolve due to factors like relocation, changes in daily routines, or the unfortunate loss of loved ones. For these reasons, proactively establishing a support network before retirement is vital.

Emotional and Mental Well-being

Retirement, freedom-filled though it may be, comes with its own set of emotional challenges. The shift from a structured work life to unscheduled days can sometimes lead to feelings of isolation, boredom, or even depression.

A strong support network can help mitigate these feelings by providing regular social interactions and fostering a sense of belonging. Friends, family, and community groups can become pillars of support that contribute to a positive mental outlook.

Practical Support

There are also plenty of practical reasons to establish a network. As you grow older, you might face health challenges or mobility issues that require assistance.

Simple tasks such as grocery shopping, attending medical appointments, or maintaining your home can become daunting without help. Having a network of trusted individuals ensures that you have access to support for these practical needs, enabling you to maintain independence longer.

Steps to Build a Strong Support Network

It's worth noting that Building a support network requires intentionality.

It's not enough to hope that friends and family will automatically be there when you need them. Here are steps to actively create and nurture this web of support:.

Identify Your Core Circle

Start by identifying the people already in your life who you can count on. These are individuals you trust and who have shown reliability over the years.

They might include family members, close friends, neighbors, or colleagues who have transitioned to being friends. Reach out to these individuals and maintain regular communication, strengthening your ties with them.

Expand Beyond Existing Relationships

While it's crucial to nurture existing relationships, expanding your network is equally important. Joining clubs, attending classes, or becoming active in community organizations can introduce you to new people who share your interests.

Look for hobby groups that align with your passions, whether that's hiking, knitting, book clubs, or even a gardening group. These settings make it easier to form connections based on shared activities.

Volunteer and Give Back

Volunteering offers a dual benefit: it allows you to contribute positively to your community, and it helps you forge new relationships.

Organizations are often in dire need of help, and giving your time can foster a strong sense of purpose and satisfaction. More importantly, this avenue introduces you to like-minded individuals, potentially forming the basis for lasting friendships.

Engage with Technology

The rise of digital technology provides new ways to stay connected. Platforms such as Facebook, WhatsApp, or Zoom make it easy to stay in touch with people both near and far.

Join online forums or groups centered around your hobbies or interests. Don't hesitate to explore resources like Meetup for local group activities or Nextdoor for neighborhood engagement. Learning to navigate these platforms can expand your social circle significantly.

Cultivate Intergenerational Relationships

While it's comforting to connect with those who share your generational experiences, intergenerational relationships provide fresh perspectives and foster learning.

Younger people can introduce you to new ideas and ways of thinking, keeping your approach to life and its challenges fresh and adaptive. Often, families can facilitate these types of connections, bridging the gap between grandparents and grandchildren, or you may find opportunities in community groups.

Nurturing and Maintaining Your Network

Let's not forget, Building a network is not a one-time effort; it requires ongoing attention and nurturing.

Here's how you can keep your relationships vibrant and mutually valuable:.

Stay Consistent

Make an effort to frequently touch base with members of your support network.

Regular meetups, phone calls, or video chats help to maintain these essential bonds. Schedule these catch-ups just as you would any other important activity.

Show Appreciation

Simple gestures of appreciation go a long way in sustaining relationships.

A quick thank-you note, an unexpected gift, or offering help in return fortifies the foundation of trusted relationships. A genuine sense of gratitude fosters warmth and makes others feel valued.

Communicate Openly

Many people don't realize this, but Open communication is the cornerstone of any strong relationship.

Be candid about your needs, expectations, and limitations. Honesty eliminates misunderstandings and builds trust, making it easier for others to support you effectively.

Adapt and Adjust

As time passes, your needs and circumstances may change, and so will the dynamics of your support network.

Be flexible and willing to adapt your relationships to meet these new circumstances. A willingness to embrace change helps ensure your network remains relevant and resilient.

Conclusion

Building a support network in retirement is not just about creating a safety net for future challenges; it's about enriching your life with meaningful connections. A robust network provides emotional sustenance, practical help, and opportunities to continually learn and grow.

It's about building a community that offers joy, understanding, and a shared experience in this new chapter of your life. By taking deliberate steps to forge these relationships, you'll enhance both your quality of life and your sense of belonging, leading to a more fulfilling and less complex retirement experience.

Chapter 19: Overcoming Common Retirement Challenges

Retiring is often envisioned as a time for relaxation, travel, and enjoying the fruits of one's labor. However, the transition from active employment to retirement can be fraught with unexpected challenges.

These challenges can range from financial concerns and health issues to emotional adjustments and maintaining social connections. Recognizing and addressing these challenges early can lead to a more fulfilling retirement.

Financial Sustainability

At first glance, One of the most prevalent concerns for retirees is ensuring their resources last throughout their retirement.

Longevity risk, or the risk of outliving your savings, is a significant worry. To tackle this challenge, it's crucial to have a clear and realistic financial plan.

Budgeting: Developing a detailed budget is fundamental. Begin by estimating your expected monthly expenses, including housing, utilities, food, healthcare, and leisure activities.

Remember to factor in inflation, which can erode purchasing power over time. Regularly reviewing and adjusting your budget to reflect changes in your lifestyle or unexpected expenses is critical to maintaining financial health.

Diversifying income: Relying solely on one source of income, such as social security or pension, can be risky.

Consider diversifying income with part-time work, investments, or rental income. If you haven't already, consult with a financial advisor who can help tailor an investment portfolio that balances risk and growth according to your needs.

Emergency Fund: Building and maintaining an emergency fund to cover unexpected expenses, such as medical emergencies or major home repairs, is essential.

Aim for a fund that covers six to twelve months' worth of living expenses, providing peace of mind and financial stability.

Healthcare and Insurance

Healthcare costs in retirement can be a substantial burden.

With advancing age comes the increased possibility of health issues that require medical attention, sometimes demanding significant financial resources.

To be honest, **Medicare and Supplemental Insurance**: Understanding Medicare and its limitations is crucial.

Consider investing in supplemental insurance policies, such as Medigap, to cover what Medicare doesn't. Conduct thorough research or consult a professional to identify the plans best suited to your needs.

Preventive Care: Embrace a proactive approach to health by engaging in preventative care.

Regular check-ups, a balanced diet, adequate exercise, and stress management can reduce the risk of developing chronic illnesses.

Long-Term Care: Consider the possibility of needing long-term care.

Policies covering long-term care expenses like nursing homes or in-home care can be expensive but worth the peace of mind if included in your retirement plan early on.

Emotional Adjustment

Retirement can trigger a profound emotional shift.

For many, identity is tied to their career, and leaving it behind can cause feelings of loss or aimlessness.

Redefining Identity: It's important to begin redefining your identity outside of your career before retirement.

Explore hobbies, volunteer work, and new learning opportunities to maintain a sense of purpose.

Let's not forget, **Setting Goals**: Setting new, achievable goals can provide structure and motivation.

Whether it's completing a personal project, taking up a new hobby, or traveling to destinations you've always dreamed of, goals can enrich your daily life with purpose.

Seeking Support: Emotional health should not be overlooked.

Stay connected with friends and family and, if needed, consider therapy to help navigate the emotional ups and downs of transitioning into retirement. Support groups for retirees can also provide a network of individuals facing similar experiences.

Maintaining Social Connections

Interestingly enough, Social isolation is a common issue among retirees due to the loss of daily interactions with colleagues and acquaintances that work provides.

Community Engagement: Engage with your community through volunteering, joining clubs, or participating in local events.

These interactions can lead to new friendships and provide a sense of belonging.

Continual Learning: Retirement is an excellent opportunity to learn something new. Consider enrolling in classes that interest you, such as art, history, or technology.

Many universities offer programs specifically designed for retirees. These settings not only provide mental stimulation but also help form new friendships.

Intergenerational Relationships: Foster relationships across generations, whether through formal mentoring programs or informal family interactions.

Sharing knowledge with younger generations can be rewarding and provides benefits for both parties involved.

Adjusting to a New Routine

The routine that work provides is difficult to replicate without effort. Creating a structured yet flexible daily routine can help bridge this gap.

Daily Planning: Start your day with a plan.

Whether it's exercise, meal planning, hobbies, or a leisurely activity, having a set of activities can keep each day exciting and purposeful.

Balancing Relaxation and Activity: It's easy to fall into a too-relaxed lifestyle upon retirement.

While downtime is important, balance it with activities that keep you engaged physically and mentally.

Legal and Estate Planning

Ensuring that your legal documents and estate plans are up to date will relieve stress for you and your loved ones.

Wills and Trusts: Make sure your will is current, reflecting your wishes and the distribution of your assets.

Trusts can also be an effective tool for managing your estate and ensuring your affairs are handled in accordance with your wishes.

Power of Attorney and Advance Directives: Assign a trusted individual as your power of attorney to make decisions if you're unable to do so yourself.

Similarly, advance health care directives ensure your medical preferences are honored should you become incapacitated.

It's worth noting that **Regular Reviews**: Reassess your legal and estate plans periodically or when significant life changes occur to ensure they remain aligned with your circumstances and wishes.

Conclusion

The key to overcoming common retirement challenges is preparation and adaptability. By proactively addressing financial, healthcare, emotional, and social aspects, retirees can embrace this new phase of life with confidence and joy.

Remember, retirement isn't just an end; it's a new beginning, full of potential and opportunity. As you navigate through this transition, maintain a mindset open to change, and be willing to seek the support and resources needed to make your retirement everything you've dreamed of.

Chapter 20: Putting It All Together: Your Simplified Retirement Plan

The path to retirement is often compared to a journey, a metaphor that aptly captures both the challenges and the joys of achieving a well-earned reprieve from years of work.

As we arrive at this pivotal chapter, our goal is to synthesize the various elements of our journey into a coherent, simplified plan that reflects your personal goals, finances, and lifestyle desires. This chapter provides you with the practical tools and strategies needed to assemble your retirement dream into an actionable and straightforward plan, free of overwhelm and complexity.

Simplification at the Core

In real life, At the heart of any efficient retirement plan is simplification. With the abundance of information and financial products available today, overcomplication can easily derail us.

To avoid the clutter, focus exclusively on strategies and investments that align with your values and desired retirement lifestyle. Review each component critically: Does this investment reflect your risk tolerance? Does it contribute to your long-term objectives? Should certain expenses be prioritized due to their substantial impact on your well-being? The art of simplification demands ruthless prioritization, but yields clarity and peace of mind.

Step 1: Define Clear Retirement Goals

A simplified retirement plan starts with crystal-clear goals. Break these goals into short-term and long-term categories.

Short-term goals might address immediate financial requirements or decisions you need to make in the next couple of years, such as paying off high-interest debt or saving for a major purchase like a downsized property. Long-term goals, on the other hand, may include travel aspirations, family engagements, or philanthropic aims. Translate these aspirations into quantifiable markers to make progress easily assessable.

I've seen this happen before: For example, if traveling is high on your priority list, identify the destinations, estimate costs, and create a savings timeline.

Crafting a concrete vision provides motivation and an actionable framework to work within.

Step 2: Financial Check-Up

The cornerstone of any retirement plan is a thorough understanding of your financial landscape.

Begin with a detailed inventory of your assets, liabilities, income streams, and regular expenditures. Once you have a firm grasp on your current condition, consider future changes that might impact this balance, such as anticipated healthcare needs or changes in family dynamics that could affect your financial responsibilities.

Let's not forget, Balancing liabilities and assets is key to ensuring financial stability.

Ensure you have sufficient liquidity for immediate needs and emergencies while maintaining a diversified investment portfolio to guard against inflation and market volatility.

Step 3: Streamline Investments

Complicated portfolios with numerous accounts and asset types can be distracting and cumbersome.

Instead, aim for simplicity by consolidating accounts and focusing on a diversified mix of low-cost index funds or ETFs that align with your risk tolerance and time horizon. Prioritize investments that offer tax efficiency and have minimal maintenance costs, reducing the time and energy you'll need to manage them.

In real life, Regularly review your investment strategy, adjusting allocations to reflect life changes or shifts in the market.

The aim is to create a self-reinforcing financial ecosystem, resilient to economic shifts and personal changes alike.

Step 4: Create a Sustainable Withdrawal Strategy

Efficiently managing your retirement funds is more critical than merely saving.

As you transition from accumulating wealth to drawing from your savings, establish a withdrawal strategy that maximizes your income while minimizing tax liabilities. Explore methods such as the 4% rule, or a tailored withdrawal rate based on your specific needs and financial situation.

Multiple income streams can provide additional security; consider Social Security, pensions, rental income, or part-time work to supplement withdrawals.

Having a diversified income pool ensures stability and guards against exhausting resources prematurely.

Step 5: Address Estate Planning and Healthcare

Though often neglected, estate planning and healthcare arrangements are fundamental to a well-rounded retirement plan.

Simplification here involves using tools like a living will, power of attorney, and clearly named beneficiaries to eliminate ambiguity and potential legal conflicts.

I've seen this happen before: Additionally, assess your healthcare coverage annually, adjusting as necessary to ensure comprehensive care that includes prescription drugs, regular check-ups, and emergency care.

Consider the benefits of long-term care insurance, especially if you anticipate needing extended assistance as you age.

Step 6: Regular Reviews and Adjustments

Your life and assets are not static; neither should your retirement plan be.

Schedule an annual review to analyze your progress towards goals, and make adjustments reflecting any life changes such as income shifts, health status, or familial obligations. A streamlined plan is not only easier to manage but also more responsive to changes, allowing for timely interventions without drastic overhauls.

Step 7: Embrace a Life-first Approach

Finally, remember that your plan exists to support the life you envision.

Don't become so fixated on financial figures and projections that you lose sight of the experiential richness retirement offers. Carefully decide what activities and relationships you want to pursue and preserve time for those.

Your financial security should facilitate, not dictate, your retirement lifestyle.

By undertaking a life-first approach, the focus aligns on using your plan as a tool to create opportunities for fulfillment, joy, and personal growth.

In Conclusion

Creating a simplified retirement plan requires effort and introspection, but the payoff is a roadmap that leads you to a financially secure and personally satisfying retirement. The methodology emphasized throughout — goal setting, financial oversight, streamlined investments, and sustainable withdrawal tactics — ensures that you remain on course no matter what unexpected twists life may present.

Your plan should be a living document, evolving alongside you and continuously serving your best interests. This holistic approach makes for not just a rewarding retirement, but a simpler, more enjoyable journey to it — crafting a future tailor-made to your aspirations, free from unnecessary complexities.

About the Author

T. S. AVINI is a writer who believes in the power of sharing life's lessons. Having faced hardship and pain, he turned to writing as a form of self-expression and healing. Today, he pours his heart into every book, aiming to help others navigate their own struggles and find strength in vulnerability.